CROSS NECKLACE

SHOPPING LIST
- 5 yards of 2 mm rust satin rat tail cord
- 2" x 3" cross pendant with attached bail
- 4 metal-lined large-hole beads (2 pearl and 2 faceted)
- 2 large-hole gold spacer beads
- large lobster claw clasp
- large jump ring
- craft glue

Approximate finished length: 25", excluding pendant

To make the necklace:
Refer to **Macramé Jewelry Basics**, page 28, before beginning your necklace.

1. Cut two 12" lengths of cord; set aside. Cut the remaining cord in three 52" lengths. Slide the pendant to the center of the cords.
2. Slide one bead onto the cords on each side of the bail.
3. Working one side of the necklace at a time and beginning approximately $1/4$" below the bead, use two outer cords to loosely tie two square knots (page 31) around the center standing cord.
4. Slide another bead onto the cords. Leaving an approximately $1 1/2$" space between the group of knots, tie another group of two square knots.
5. Slide a spacer bead onto the cords. Trim the cord ends $9 1/2$" from the last knot.
6. Repeat Steps 3-5 for the opposite side of the necklace.
7. Finish the cord ends (page 32) using the jump ring on one end and the lobster claw clasp on the other end.

NUGGET NECKLACE

SHOPPING LIST

- 6 yards of yellow braiding cord
- 3 large silver nugget beads
- 2 large-hole decorative beads
- decorative "S" clasp
- medium jump ring
- craft glue

Approximate finished length: 21"

To make the necklace:
Refer to **Macramé Jewelry Basics**, *page 28, before beginning your necklace.*

1. Cut two 12" lengths of cord; set aside. Cut the remaining cord into five 38" lengths. Slide one nugget to the center of one cord.
2. Holding two cords together, fold in half. Knot the center of the lengths around the single cord on one side of the nugget bead.
3. Working one side of the necklace at a time, use two outer cords on each side to tie a square knot (page 31) around the center standing cord.
4. Slide a nugget bead onto the standing cord; tie four square knots.
5. Holding all the cords together, slide a decorative bead on the cords. Trim the cord ends 8 1/2" from the last knot.
6. Repeat Steps 3-5 with the remaining cords, nugget, and bead for the opposite side of the necklace.
7. Finish the cord ends (page 32) using the jump ring on one end and the "S" clasp on the other end.

Macramé Jewelry

Learn a few simple knots and discover the thrill of creating one-of-a-kind jewelry. Once you see how fast and easy it is, you'll be making colorful accessories for all your favorite outfits, as well as gifts to please your friends.

LEISURE ARTS, INC. • Little Rock, Arkansas

PENDANT NECKLACE

SHOPPING LIST

- [ ] 1 yard of 2 mm royal blue satin rat tail cord
- [ ] 5 yards of purple braiding cord
- [ ] 1" x 1¾" confetti-filled pendant with jump ring
- [ ] metal and rhinestone large-hole barrel bead
- [ ] 2 metal and rhinestone large-hole spacer beads
- [ ] medium lobster claw clasp
- [ ] medium jump ring
- [ ] craft glue

Approximate finished length: 30", excluding pendant

To make the necklace:

*Refer to **Macramé Jewelry Basics**, page 28, before beginning your necklace.*

1. Cut two 12" lengths of purple cord; set aside. Cut the remaining purple cord into two equal lengths. Match the centers of the purple and blue cords. Slide the pendant to the center of the cords.
2. Slide the barrel bead onto the cords and down to the jump ring.
3. Working one side of the necklace at a time and beginning approximately ⅜" below the bead, use two purple cords to make three square knots (page 31) around the blue rat tail standing cord.
4. Leaving an approximately ⅜" space between each group of knots, make five additional groups of three square knots.
5. Slide a spacer bead onto the cords; tie an overhand knot (page 30). Trim the cords 10½" from the overhand knot.
6. Repeat Steps 3-5 for the opposite side of the necklace.
7. Finish the cord ends (page 32) using the jump ring on one end and the lobster claw clasp on the other end.

PEARL & RHINESTONE CHOKER

SHOPPING LIST

- [ ] 6 yards of black braiding cord that will fit through the beads
- [ ] 120 6 mm round white pearl beads
- [ ] 16" of black metal and rhinestone link chain with eyelet ends
- [ ] toggle clasp
- [ ] craft glue
- [ ] 2 pairs of chain-nose pliers

Approximate finished length: 17$\frac{1}{2}$"

To make the choker:
Refer to Macramé Jewelry Basics, page 28, before beginning your choker.

1. Attach the toggle clasp (page 29) to the ends of the chain.
2. Beginning with the center of the cord below the first rhinestone on one end, tie a square knot (page 31) around the chain.
3. Slide one bead onto each cord; tie a square knot around the chain in the space below the next rhinestone.
4. Continue adding beads and tying square knots in the spaces between the rhinestones until you reach the last rhinestone; knot the ends. Place a drop of glue on the cord ends. When the glue is dry, trim the cord ends.

SILVER MEDALLION BRACELET

SHOPPING LIST

- 3 yards of 2 mm grey rat tail cord
- decorative metal medallion with eyelets on opposite sides
- decorative lobster claw clasp
- 2 medium jump rings
- 2 pairs of chain-nose pliers
- craft glue

To make the bracelet:

*Refer to **Macramé Jewelry Basics**, page 28, before beginning your bracelet.*

1. Using a jump ring, attach the lobster claw clasp to the medallion (page 29). Measure your wrist and decide how loose or tight you want your bracelet; subtract the clasp and medallion length.
2. Cut a 12" length of cord; set aside. Cut the remaining cord into one 24" length and one 72" length. Match the centers of the cords. Slide the medallion to the center of the cords.
3. The two short cord ends are the standing cords that the knots are tied around. Use the long cord ends to tie square knots (page 31) around the two standing cords until the bracelet is equal to the measurement determined in Step 1. Trim the cord ends 1" from the last knot.
4. Finish the cord ends (page 32) using the jump ring.

BUCKLE BRACELET

SHOPPING LIST

- 4 1/4 yards of 2 mm coral satin rat tail cord
- 7/8" x 1" rhinestone buckle
- metal-lined large-hole rhinestone bead
- craft glue

Fig. 1

To make the bracelet:

Refer to Macramé Jewelry Basics, page 28, before beginning your bracelet.

1. Cut a 3 3/4" length of cord; set aside. Cut the remaining cord in two 36" lengths and one 72" length.
2. Match the centers of the lengths. Fold the lengths in half. Keeping the long lengths flat and side by side, wrap the 3 3/4" cord length around the folded cords 1 1/4" below the fold *(Fig. 1)*; glue the ends on back.
3. Slide the buckle on the cord lengths.
4. Use the two long cords to loosely tie square knots (page 31) around the four short standing cords approximately 1/4" apart until the bracelet is the right length.
5. Slide the bead onto the cords; tie an overhand knot (page 30) in each cord below the bead; trim the cord ends.

CHARM BRACELET

SHOPPING LIST

- [ ] 3 yards of 2 mm fuchsia satin rat tail cord
- [ ] 2 metal large-hole beads
- [ ] approximately 26 assorted bead charms (purchased as an assortment with jump rings attached)
- [ ] 2 metal cones
- [ ] toggle clasp
- [ ] 2 small jump rings
- [ ] 24 gauge wire
- [ ] craft glue
- [ ] 2 pairs of chain-nose pliers

To make the bracelet:
*Refer to **Macramé Jewelry Basics**, page 28, before beginning your bracelet.*

1. Measure your wrist and decide how loose or tight you want your bracelet; subtract $4^{3}/_{4}$" for beaded area, cones, and clasp. Divide this measurement by two to determine the length of each knotted area of the bracelet.
2. Cut the cord into two 36" lengths and two 18" lengths. Holding two short cords together, thread the charms onto the center of the cords. Thread one bead on each end of the cords. Push all the bead charms close together between the two beads and glue the beads in place on the cords.
3. The two cords holding the beads are the standing cords that the knots are tied around. Working one side of the bracelet at a time, knot the long cords around the standing cords. Tie square knots (page 31) around the standing cords until the knots are equal to the measurement determined in Step 1.
4. Repeat Step 3 with the remaining long cord for the opposite side of the bracelet.
5. Holding ends together, tightly wrap a 6" wire length around the cords *(Fig. 1)* close to the knots. Trim the cord ends to $^{1}/_{2}$" long.

Fig. 1

6. Thread the wire end through a cone and pull until the wrapped cord ends are drawn into the cone *(Fig. 2)*. Trim the wire to $^{1}/_{4}$". Make a loop in the wire (page 29).

Fig. 2

7. Repeat Steps 5-6 for the other side of the bracelet.
8. Use the jump rings (page 29) to attach the toggle clasp to the wire loops.

JOSEPHINE KNOT BRACELET

SHOPPING LIST
- 4 yards of 2 mm yellow satin rat tail cord
- large black metal springring clasp
- large black metal "S" clasp

To make the bracelet:

Refer to Macramé Jewelry Basics, page 28, before beginning your bracelet.

1. Attach the "S" clasp to the springring clasp. Measure your wrist and decide how loose or tight you want your bracelet; subtract the clasp length.
2. Cut the cord into two 72" lengths. Holding the cords together, fold the lengths in half. Attach the center of the cords to the springring clasp with a lark's head knot (page 30).
3. Beginning about 1 1/2" from clasp, tie a Josephine knot (page 31). Spacing the knots about 3/8" apart, tie Josephine knots until the bracelet is equal to the measurement determined in Step 1.
4. Holding the cords together and catching the "S" clasp in the knot, tie an overhead knot (page 30). Trim the cord ends to 2". Tie an overhand knot in each cord end.

GREEN BLING BRACELET

SHOPPING LIST

- ☐ 4 yards of green braiding cord
- ☐ green glass seed beads (we used 56 for our 9" bracelet)
- ☐ rhinestone chain with rhinestone chain ends
- ☐ toggle clasp with attached jump rings
- ☐ 2 pairs of chain-nose pliers
- ☐ wire cutters
- ☐ craft glue

To make the bracelet:

*Refer to **Macramé Jewelry Basics**, page 28, before beginning your bracelet.*

1. Attach the two parts of the toggle clasp together. Measure your wrist and decide how loose or tight you want your bracelet; subtract the clasp length. Cut the rhinestone chain to the determined measurement.
2. Attach a rhinestone chain end to the last stone on each end of the chain **(Fig. 1)**.

Fig. 1

3. Use jump rings (page 29) to attach the toggle clasp to the chain ends.
4. Beginning with the center of the cord below the rhinestone chain end, knot the cord around the chain. Tie a square knot (page 31) in the space below the next rhinestone.
5. Slide one bead onto each cord next to a rhinestone; tie a square knot around the chain in the space below the next rhinestone.
6. Continue adding beads and tying square knots in the spaces between the rhinestones until you reach the last rhinestone. Knot the ends between the last rhinestone and the rhinestone end. Place a drop of glue on the cord ends. When the glue is dry, trim the ends.

BEADED CUFF

> **SHOPPING LIST**
> - 10 yards of purple braiding cord that will fit through the beads
> - grey 8 mm pearl beads (we used 29 for our 8" bracelet)
> - 5/8" diameter shank-style button

To make the bracelet:

Refer to Macramé Jewelry Basics, page 28, before beginning your bracelet.

1. Measure your wrist and decide how loose or tight you want your cuff; add 1/2".
2. Cut four 78" lengths and three 15" lengths of braiding cord. Holding the ends together, tie an overhand knot (page 30) about 1/2" from one end.
3. Arrange the cords as shown in **Fig. 1**.

Fig. 1

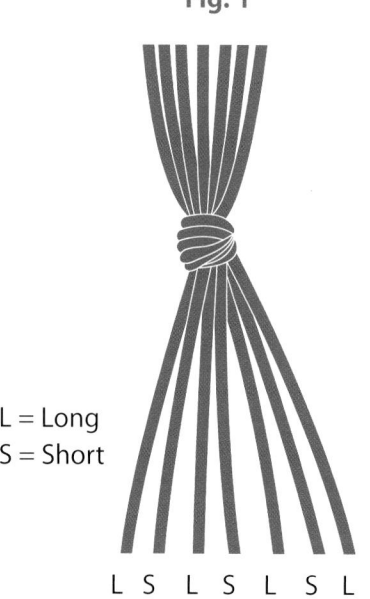

L = Long
S = Short

L S L S L S L

4. The knots are tied using a group of three cords. In a group, the short cord is the standing cord that the knots are tied around. Using three cords on the left side (**Fig. 2**), tie three square knots (page 31).

Fig. 2

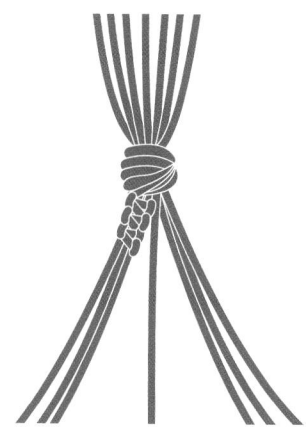

5. Using three cords on the right side, tie three square knots.
6. Using three cords in the center, tie three square knots (**Fig. 3**).

Fig. 3

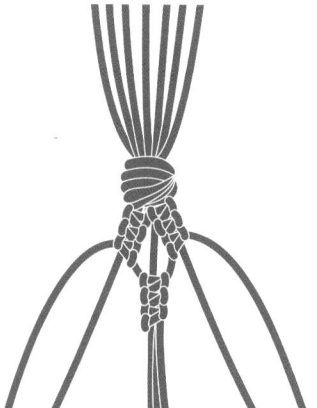

7. Slide a bead on the standing cord of the left outer group. Using three cords on the left side, tie three square knots.
8. Slide a bead on the standing cord of the right outer group. Using three cords on the right side, tie three square knots. Slide a bead on the standing cord in the center; tie three square knots.
9. Ending with three square knots on the outer cords, repeat Steps 7-8 until the bracelet is equal to the measurement determined in Step 1. Slide the button on the inner three cords. Tie an overhand knot with all cords; trim the cord ends about 1/2" from the knot.

RIBBON BRACELET

SHOPPING LIST

- 3 yards of black braiding cord
- 1/2 yard of 5/8" wide grey grosgrain ribbon
- 16 4 mm silver beads
- crystal and metal oval link
- oval rings from two toggle clasps
- "S" clasp
- craft glue

To make the bracelet:

Refer to Macramé Jewelry Basics, page 28, before beginning your bracelet.

1. Measure your wrist and decide how loose or tight you want your bracelet. Cut the ribbon length and two lengths of cord to the determined measurement.
2. Cut the remaining braid in half. Use a lark's head knot (page 30) to attach each piece to opposite ends of the oval link.
3. Center the link over the two lengths of cord cut in Step 1. Tape the link and cords down. Using the cords attached to the link as the standing cords, tie two square knots (page 31) on each side of the link.
4. Center the link and knots on the ribbon length. Glue the knots and standing cords to the ribbon length; allow to dry.
5. Using the ribbon as the standing cords and sliding a bead on after each knot, tie five square knots on each side of bracelet. Allow the ribbon to gather slightly when knotting.
6. Tie three square knots on each side of bracelet. Secure cords on back of bracelet with a knot. Place a drop of glue on the knot; allow to dry. Trim the cord ends.
7. Add "S" clasp to one toggle piece. Place the toggle clasp pieces on each end of ribbon; fold ribbon ends 3/4" to wrong side and glue.

DISCO BALL BEAD BRACELET

SHOPPING LIST

Supplies and instructions given are for making one bracelet.

- ☐ 6 yards of braiding cord
- ☐ 5 14 mm resin disco ball beads
- ☐ toggle clasp
- ☐ craft glue

To make the bracelet:

Refer to Macramé Jewelry Basics, page 28, before beginning your bracelet.

1. Attach the two parts of the toggle clasp together. Measure your wrist and decide how loose or tight you want your bracelet; subtract the clasp length. Divide this measurement by two.
2. Cut two 12" lengths of braiding cord; set aside. Cut the remaining braiding cord into four 48" lengths.
3. Tape the center of the cords down. The two cords in the center are the standing cords that the knots are tied around. Slide one bead to the center of the standing cord lengths.
4. Use the outer cords to tie three square knots (page 31) around the two center standing cords.
5. Thread a bead on the standing cords. Tie three square knots and slide on another bead. Continue making square knots until the bracelet equals the measurement determined in Step 1.
6. Repeat Steps 4-5 for the other side of the bracelet.
7. Trim the cord ends to 1". Finish the cord ends (page 32) using the toggle clasp.

CENTER STONE BRACELET

SHOPPING LIST

- 4 yards of 2 mm blue satin rat tail cord
- ½ yard of blue braiding cord
- 9 mm x 12 mm faceted glass bead
- 2 glass seed beads
- 1¼" diameter silver metal ring
- 2 metal cones
- toggle clasp
- 24 gauge wire
- round-nose pliers

To make each bracelet:

Refer to Macramé Jewelry Basics, page 28, before beginning your bracelet.

1. Measure your wrist and decide how loose or tight you want your bracelet; subtract 3½" for ring, cones, and clasp. Divide this measurement by two.
2. Slide the beads to the center of the braiding cord *(Fig. 1)*.

Fig. 1

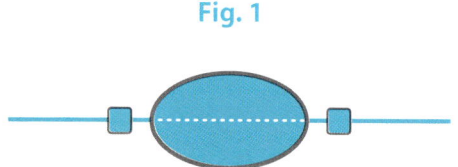

3. The braiding cord is the standing cord that the knots are tied around. Place the braiding cord across the ring with the beads centered in the ring.
4. Cut the rat tail cord in half. Attach the center of one rat tail cord length to each side of the ring with a lark's head knot (page 30), over the braiding cord.
5. Use the rat tail cord on one side of the ring to make square knots (page 31) around the standing cord until the knots are equal to the measurement determined in Step 1.
6. Repeat Step 5 with the remaining cords for the opposite side of the bracelet.
7. Holding the ends together, tightly wrap a 6" wire length around the cords *(Fig. 2)* close to the knots. Trim the cord ends to ½".

Fig. 2

8. Thread the wire end through a cone and pull until the wrapped cord ends are drawn into the cone *(Fig. 3)*. Trim the wire to ¼". Making a loop in the wire (page 29), attach one end of the toggle clasp.

Fig. 3

9. Repeat Steps 7-8 for the other side of the bracelet.

LADDER BRACELET

SHOPPING LIST
- 2½ yards of 2 mm yellow satin rat tail cord
- 9 assorted large-hole beads
- craft glue

To make the bracelet:
Refer to Macramé Jewelry Basics, page 28, before beginning your bracelet.

1. Cut a 24" length of cord; set aside. Cut the remaining cord into two 30" lengths. Tie an overhand knot (page 30) in one end of each cord.
2. Holding the cords together, tie another overhand knot about 3" from the knotted ends.
3. Leaving about a ½" space from the knot and inserting each cord from opposite sides of the bead, thread a bead onto the cords *(Fig. 1)*.

Fig. 1

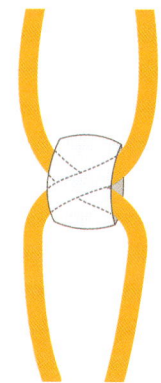

4. Leaving about ½" between each bead, repeat Step 3 to thread the beads onto the cords.
5. Holding the cords together, tie another overhand knot about ½" from the last bead. Trim the cord ends about 3½" from the knot. Tie overhand knots in each cord end.
6. For the sliding closure, place the 24" length of cord underneath the ends of the bracelet *(Fig. 2)*. Refer to **Figs. 3-5** to tie 4 square knots (page 31).

Fig. 2

Fig. 3

Fig. 4

18   www.leisurearts.com

Fig. 5

7. Tie a tight knot on the underside of the closure. Apply glue to the knot; allow to dry. After glue is dry, trim the cord ends. Apply glue to the newly trimmed ends to prevent fraying; allow to dry.
8. Tighten the bracelet by pulling on the knotted ends. Loosen the bracelet by pulling on the bracelet.

BLUE BEAD BRACELET

SHOPPING LIST

- ☐ 4 yards of 2 mm royal blue satin rat tail cord
- ☐ 3 metal-lined large-hole glass beads
- ☐ 2 large-hole spacer beads

Approximate finished length: 8"

To make the bracelet:

*Refer to **Macramé Jewelry Basics**, page 28, before beginning your bracelet.*

1. Cut the cord into two 72" lengths. Holding the cords together at the center, tie an overhand knot (page 30) forming a ³/₄" loop.
2. Use the outer cords to tie six square knots (page 31) around the two center standing cords. Slide one glass bead on the standing cords. Tie another square knot.
3. Slide one glass bead and two spacer beads on cords.
4. Tie one square knot and slide on the remaining glass bead. Tie six square knots.
5. Holding the cords together, tie an overhand knot; trim the ends to about 1".

BLACK BLING BEAD EARRINGS

SHOPPING LIST

- ⅝ yard of 2 mm black satin rat tail cord
- 2 metal-lined large-hole rhinestone beads
- 2 large-hole silver spacer beads
- 2 tubular cord ends
- 2 earring wires
- jewel glue
- 2 pairs of chain-nose pliers

Approximate finished length: 2"

To make each earring:

1. Cut a 10" length of rat tail cord. Insert each end of the cord from opposite sides of a rhinestone bead *(Fig. 1)*.

Fig. 1

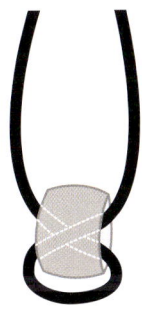

2. Slide one spacer bead onto the cord ends.
3. Trim the cord ends to 1½" *(Fig. 2)*. Glue the ends into the tubular cord end.

Fig. 2

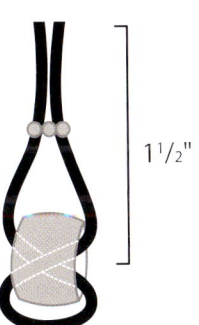

1½"

4. Attach an earring wire to the cord end (page 29).

PINK AND PEARL EARRINGS

SHOPPING LIST

- [ ] 2 yards braiding cord
- [ ] 2 rhinestone spacer beads
- [ ] 2 pink faceted glass beads
- [ ] 2 flat disc-shaped metal beads
- [ ] 2 metal barrel beads
- [ ] 2 6 mm pearl beads
- [ ] 24 gauge wire
- [ ] 2 earring wires
- [ ] craft glue
- [ ] round-nose pliers
- [ ] 2 pairs of chain-nose pliers

Approximate finished length: 2¼"

To make each earring:
Refer to *Macramé Jewelry Basics*, page 28, before beginning your earrings.

1. Cut two 18" lengths of braiding cord.
2. Leaving an approximately 1" tail, tie one length to the center of another length *(Fig. 1)*. Place a drop of glue on the knot; allow to dry. Do not trim tail at this time.

Fig. 1

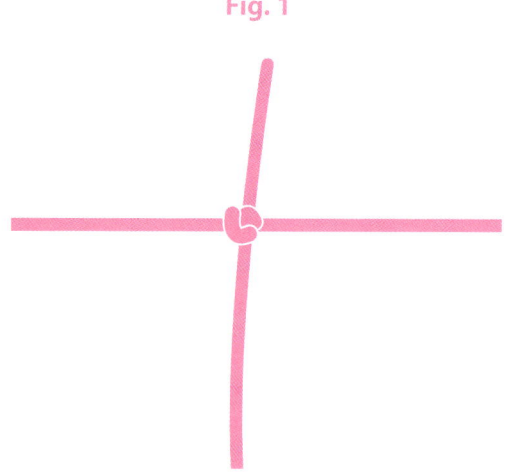

3. Tape the tail down. Slide a rhinestone spacer bead and a glass bead on the center cord. The center cord is the standing cord that the knots are tied around. Make a square knot (page 31) below the glass bead.
4. Slide a disc-shaped metal bead onto the cords and make 3 square knots.
5. Holding the ends together, tightly wrap a 6" wire length around the cords *(Fig. 2)* close to the knots. Add a drop of glue; allow to dry. Trim the cord ends to ½" long.

Fig. 2

6. Thread the wire end through a barrel bead and a pearl bead and pull until the wrapped cord ends are drawn into the barrel bead *(Fig. 3)*. Trim the wire to ¼". Make a loop with the wire (page 29).

Fig. 3

7. Attach the earring wire to the loop (page 29). Trim the tail close to the knot.

BLUE EARRINGS

SHOPPING LIST
- ⁵⁄₈ yard of 2 mm royal blue satin rat tail cord
- 2 large-hole embossed metal beads
- 2 large-hole spacer beads
- 2 decorative cord ends
- 2 earring wires
- jewel glue
- 2 pairs of chain-nose pliers

Approximate finished length: 2"

To make each earring:

1. Cut a 10" length of rat tail cord. Insert each end of the cord from opposite sides of a large-hole bead *(Fig. 1)*.

Fig. 1

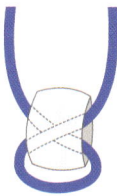

2. Slide one spacer bead onto the cord ends.
3. Trim the cord ends to 1" *(Fig. 2)*. Glue the ends into the decorative cord end.

Fig. 2

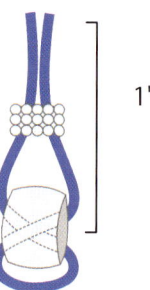

4. Attach an earring wire (page 29) to the cord end.

BEAD CAGE EARRINGS

SHOPPING LIST

- ☐ ⅝ yard of 2 mm variegated pastel satin rat tail cord
- ☐ 2 decorative metal large-hole spacer beads
- ☐ 2 rhinestone large-hole spacer beads
- ☐ 2 15 mm x 10.5 mm teardrop hinged cages
- ☐ 2 8 mm beads to fit in cage
- ☐ 2 tubular cord ends
- ☐ 2 earring wires
- ☐ jewel glue
- ☐ 2 pairs of chain-nose pliers

Approximate finished length: 3"

To make each earring:

1. Cut a 10" length of rat tail cord. Place one bead in a bead cage; close. Slide the cage to the center of the rat tail cord length.
2. Slide one rhinestone spacer bead and one metal spacer bead onto the cord ends.
3. Trim the cord ends to 1½" *(Fig. 1)*. Glue the ends into the tubular cord end.

Fig. 1

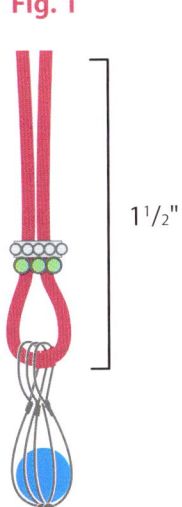

4. Attach an earring wire (page 29) to the cord end.

TRI-COLOR BEAD EARRINGS

SHOPPING LIST

- [ ] 4 yards of brown braiding cord
- [ ] 2 silver, 2 gold, and 2 copper 14 mm faceted beads
- [ ] 2 silver tubular metal cord ends
- [ ] 2 earring wires
- [ ] jewel glue
- [ ] 2 pairs of chain-nose pliers

Approximate finished length: 3"

To make each earring:

Refer to **Macramé Jewelry Basics**, page 28, before beginning your earrings.

1. Cut two 36" lengths of braiding cord.
2. Tie one length to the center of another length *(Fig. 1)*. Place a drop of glue on the knot; allow to dry. Do not trim tail at this time.
3. Tape the tail down. Slide a silver bead on the center cord. The center cord is the standing cord that the knots are tied around. Make a square knot (page 31) below the bead.
4. Slide a gold bead onto the cords and make another square knot.
5. Slide a bronze bead onto the cords and make a square knot.
6. Trim the cord ends 1/2" from the knot *(Fig. 2)*. Glue the ends into the tubular cord end.
7. Attach an earring wire to the cord end (page 29).

Fig. 1

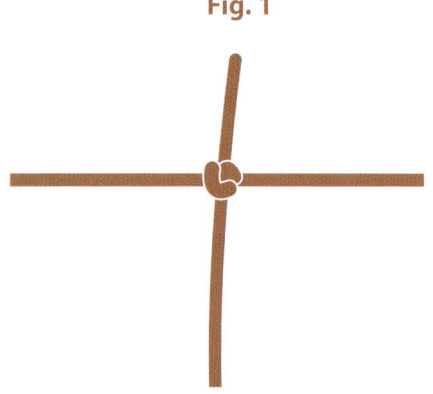

Fig. 2

MACRAMÉ JEWELRY BASICS

FIBERS
The main supply needed for macrame jewelry is the cord used for knotting the designs. There are all kinds of cords available but our projects feature satin rat tail cord and braiding cord.

FINDINGS
Findings are the components used to assemble jewelry.

BEADS
Beads come in all sizes, shapes, colors, finishes, and materials and can be used for macrame jewelry.

TOOLS

Chain-nose pliers have rounded, tapered jaws and a flat interior surface that will not mar wire. These pliers are used for reaching into tight places, gripping objects, opening and closing jump rings, and bending wire.

Round-nose pliers have round jaws that are useful for making loops and bending wire smoothly.

Wire cutters are used to cut small gauge wire, head pins, and eye pins.

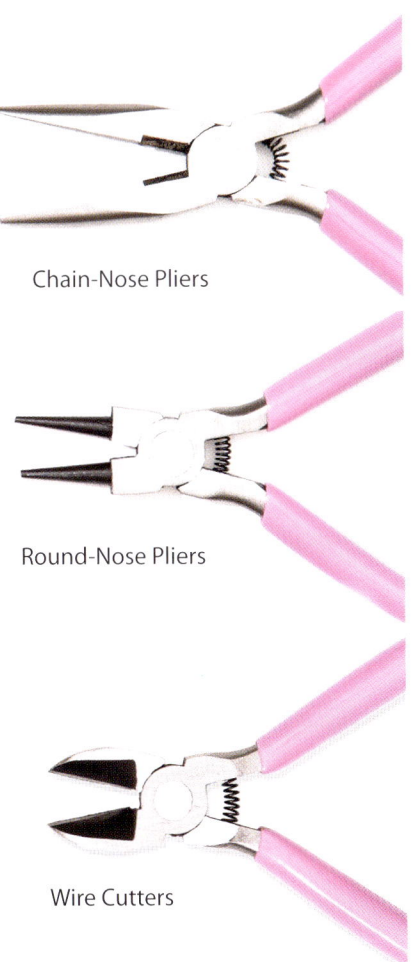

Chain-Nose Pliers

Round-Nose Pliers

Wire Cutters

TECHNIQUES
Using Jump Rings

Pick up a jump ring with the chain-nose pliers. With a second pair of chain-nose pliers, gently hold the other side of the ring. Open the ring by pulling one pair of pliers toward you while pushing the other away *(Fig. 1)*.

Fig. 1

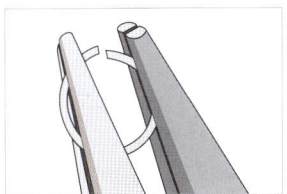

Close the ring by pushing and pulling the pliers in opposite directions, bringing the ring ends back together.

Making Loops on Wire

Using chain-nose pliers, bend the wire at a 90° angle *(Fig. 2)*. Grasp the very tip of the wire with the round-nose pliers. Turn the pliers and bend the wire into a loop *(Fig. 3)*. Release the pliers. Straighten or twist the loop further if necessary.

Fig. 2

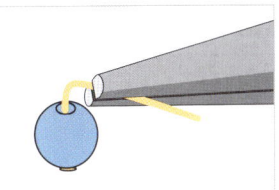

Fig. 3

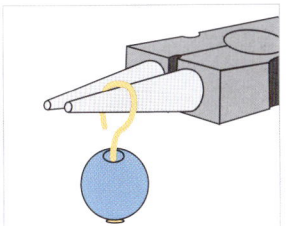

TYING KNOTS
Before You Start
- The cords should be anchored while you are knotting. Tape the starting end to the work surface.
- Support cords are cords that knots are worked around. These cords should be taut as you work. You can tape these down to the work surface if desired.

Lark's Head Knot
Fold the cord in half. Place the loop through the ring, link, or clasp. Bring the cord ends through the loop and pull to tighten *(Fig. 4)*.

Fig. 4

Overhand Knot
For an overhand knot with cut ends, hold the cords together and tie an overhand knot *(Fig. 5)* near one end.

Fig. 5

For an overhand knot with a loop end, fold the cords in half and tie an overhand knot *(Fig. 6)* near the folded end.

Fig. 6

Square Knot

Use the outer cords to make square knots *(Figs. 7-8)* around the support cord(s). When tightening, always pull the cord up or away from you.

Josephine Knot

Use the cords to make a Josephine knot *(Figs. 9-12)*.

Fig. 7

Fig. 8

Fig. 9

Fig. 10

Fig. 11

Fig. 12

FINISHING CORD ENDS

1. Holding the cords together and leaving 1" tails, thread the cords through the jump ring or clasp and fold over *(Fig. 13)*.

Fig. 13

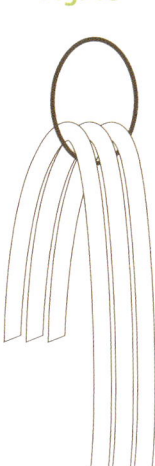

2. Form a loop with one 12" length of the cord. Wrap the cord around the folded cords 4-5 times. Bring the end through the loop *(Fig. 14)*. Pull firmly on the opposite end of the cord until the loop disappears.

Fig. 14

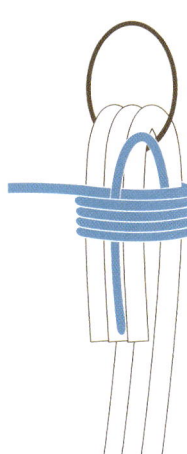

3. Place a drop of glue on the knot. When the glue is dry, trim the cord ends *(Fig. 15)*.

Fig. 15

Copyright © 2013 by Leisure Arts, Inc., 5701 Ranch Drive, Little Rock, AR 72223-9633. All rights reserved. This publication is protected under federal copyright laws. Reproduction or distribution of this publication or any other Leisure Arts publication, including publications which are out of print, is prohibited unless specifically authorized. This includes, but is not limited to, any form of reproduction or distribution on or through the Internet, including posting, scanning, or e-mail transmission.

We have made every effort to ensure that these instruction are accurate and complete. We cannot, however, be responsible for human error, typographical mistakes, or variations in individual work.

Production Team: Designer – Patti Wallenfang; Design Assistant – Kelly Reider; Technical Writer – Lisa Lancaster; Technical Associate – Mary Sullivan Hutcheson; Editorial Writer – Susan Frantz Wiles; Senior Graphic Artist – Lora Puls; Graphic Artists – Jessica Bramlett, Kara Darling, and Becca Snider Tally ; Photostylist – Lori Wenger; Photographer – Jason Masters.